ABIGAIL ADAMS

written and illustrated by ALEXANDRA WALLNER

HOLIDAY HOUSE / New York

The painting of Weymouth Parsonage on the dedication page
is based on a folk artist's sketch, c. 1765–1800.

Library of Congress Cataloging-in-Publication Data
Wallner, Alexandra.
Abigail Adams / by Alexandra Wallner. — 1st ed.
p. cm.
Summary: A biography of Abigail Adams,
wife of second United States President John Adams,
and a dedicated wife and mother who spoke up
against slavery and for women's rights.
ISBN 0-8234-1442-6
1. Adams, Abigail, 1744–1818—Juvenile literature.
2. Presidents' spouses—United States—Biography—Juvenile literature.
3. Adams, John, 1735–1826—Juvenile literature.
[1. Adams, Abigail, 1744–1818. 2. First ladies. 3. Women—Biography.
4. Adams, John, 1735–1826.] I. Title.
E322.1.A38 W355 2001
973.4'4'092—dc21
[B]   00-023149

Abigail Smith was born on November 11, 1744, to the Reverend William and Elizabeth Quincy Smith. Abigail lived with her parents, her brother, William, and her two sisters, Mary and Elizabeth, near Boston in Weymouth, Massachusetts.

Abigail always asked many questions. She was curious about everything and wondered what the world outside her family was like.

As Abigail grew older, she begged to go to school, but her mother said no. Only her brother was allowed to go. Abigail thought this was terribly unfair. She was taught reading and writing at home, but her mother felt housework was more important.

It was the first time Abigail knew that girls did not have equal rights.

Abigail spent many hours reading in her father's library. She would also sit there listening to visitors talk about politics and local events. The library became her school.

When Abigail was a teenager, she visited relatives in Boston. After she returned home, she wrote to her new friends, sharing her thoughts and feelings. Writing letters became important to her.

At age seventeen, Abigail met a young lawyer named John Adams. She liked him because he was curious, spoke his mind, and knew a lot about the world. When apart, they wrote each other many letters. Soon she called him "Dearest Friend."

As a colonial woman, Abigail knew her future depended on her husband. She felt John respected her feelings. When he asked her to marry him, she said yes.

John and Abigail were married on October 25, 1764, and went to live on his farm in Braintree, Massachusetts. Their first child, Abigail ("Nabby"), was born on July 14, 1765.

At this time, the British Stamp Act required a tax on American legal documents. The colonists hated this law, but they had no voice in their government. John wanted to help the colonists. He soon became a well-known spokesman against the British and was often away from home.

At the farm, Abigail managed the animals, land, and money. She did a good job, but she was often lonely. Writing letters made her feel better. So did the birth of their first son, John Quincy, on July 17, 1767.

In 1768, Abigail, John, and their children moved to Boston. Abigail liked living in the city. She visited friends, shopped, and read newspapers. She learned more about current events. Abigail and John discussed being ruled by England with friends. She believed more strongly than ever in the cause of freedom.

John and Abigail kept working for liberty as their family grew. On December 28, 1768, their second daughter, Suzanna, was born. She died a year later. Their son Charles was born on May 29, 1770.

John was elected to the Massachusetts legislature, which was fighting against British rule. Abigail was proud of him and wrote, "[I was] very willing to share in all that was to come."

To boycott goods that carried British taxes, Abigail and other colonial women wove their own cloth and brewed "liberty tea" from herbs. Women were becoming important to the colonists' cause.

On September 15, 1772, Abigail and John's son Thomas was born.

A year later, colonists called Sons of Liberty disguised themselves as Indians and broke the law by dumping crates of tea from British ships into Boston Harbor. This protest, known as the Boston Tea Party, made Abigail afraid of what the British might do in response. She took her children back to Braintree for safety.

In 1775, the battles of Lexington and Concord marked the beginning of the Revolutionary War. Many people fled Boston, afraid the city might be attacked. Some passed Abigail's farm. She crowded them into her house and barn, giving them food and shelter. She wrote, "The house is a Scene of Confusion."

Abigail saw the terrible Battle of Bunker Hill. She wrote of it to John. He showed her letters to General George Washington and other leaders. Through her words, they felt people's suffering.

Abigail thought this would be a good time to speak up about her beliefs. She felt that a country fighting for independence should not have slaves. Also, women should have the same rights as men. She wrote these requests to John, hoping he would include them in the laws he was helping to write.

John replied, "I cannot but laugh."

Abigail was bitterly disappointed to read John's answer.

On July 18, 1776, the Declaration of Independence was read in Boston.
It stated that the colonies were free from British rule. But sadly it ignored
the freedom of slaves and the rights of women.

In 1777, John was asked to go to France to represent the United States.

John Quincy went, too. Abigail sent her ten-year-old son letters
full of advice: watch your temper, tell the truth, keep a promise.
  In charge again at home, Abigail sent her daughter Nabby to
school in Boston to get a good education.

John returned home, but he left again for France with both John Quincy and Charles. John and Abigail missed each other, and in 1784, she joined him.

Abigail believed that helping her husband was her most important job. She gave wonderful dinner parties and talked about politics. Later, John was made ambassador to England.

In 1788, John and Abigail came back to cheering crowds in Boston Harbor. The next year, George Washington was elected the first president of the United States, and John Adams was elected vice president.

Sometimes Abigail joined John in Philadelphia, the capital of the United States at that time. But often she was sick and stayed at home on their new farm, Peacefield. Abigail taught a black servant reading and writing when he was not allowed to go to the local school.

John was elected president in 1796. As First Lady, Abigail
entertained many important people. She had little time for herself.
When the capital was moved to Washington, D.C., Abigail
was the first president's wife to live in the White House.

She thought the unfinished mansion cold, drafty, and uncomfortable. Once she had the family's laundry hung in the big main conference room. She wrote, "I am sick, sick, sick of public life."

When John was not reelected in 1800, Abigail was glad to return home.

Abigail and John enjoyed many years with friends and family. Because Abigail had managed their money well for so long, they lived comfortably.

Abigail died on October 28, 1818. She had believed her most important role was that of wife and mother. But she also spoke up against slavery and for women's rights. She wrote, "I will never consent to have our sex considered in an inferior point of light."

AUTHOR'S NOTE

More than two thousand of Abigail's letters have survived,
showing her spirit and courage.

Her son John Quincy became the sixth president
of the United States in 1824.

Part of Braintree was renamed Quincy during Abigail's lifetime.
Peacefield is now a museum.

The parsonage in Weymouth where Abigail was born
is also a museum.